*Dedicated to all who accept and respect
feelings!*

It's OK!

(To be Hopeless!)

Smieetaa Dimber

BookLeaf Publishing

India | USA | UK

Presentation by *BookLeaf Publishing*

Web: www.bookleafpub.com

E-mail: info@bookleafpub.com

ISBN: 9789363311749

First edition 2024

Gratitude!

Thanks to each and everyone who motivates me to write! Special thanks to Rucha Utpat for creating illustrations for some of the thoughts.

PREFACE

After FaceIT, I was looking for an opportunity to publish one more book. Though there are multiple concepts and stories that I did like to share, I thought of exploring my skills in writing poems based on some theme. Unrequited love, or one-sided connections struck me when I saw a video where Lord Krishna explains about three types of attractions. He explains about Bhav, Abhav and Prabhav. A person could be attracted to someone due to some emotion, or absence of some emotion or he/she may be influenced by some positives in oneself. In all cases, it is very important for the feeling bearer to accept and respect that emotion. As well, it is important for the other person to respect in all cases rather than exploit. I interpreted or rather connected every relation that we have. The collection of poems is focused on one-sided love, which is the theme of this book. Ignoring the dilution that we have seen due to the mediums around and accepting the real-life stories, I have spawned incidents around it! I hope you all like them.

A Hiiiiii

I saw him walking towards me,
I wore my glasses to confirm thee,

Trust me, in that fleeting moment,
My heartbeat skipped, lost in torment.

His eyes met mine, a silent plea,
A world of words that couldn't be.

He smiled and softly said, "Hi,"
My heart soared, asking "why."

Gathering pieces of my fractured soul,
I whispered back, "Hi," trying to be whole.

He turned away, the moment passed,
Leaving me with a feeling that would last.

In the silence, my heart still yearned,
For a love that never truly returned.

Hide and Seek

No matter how much we talk, how much we meet,
In this game of hide and seek, our hearts beat.

Through whispered conversations and stolen glances,
We dance in the shadows, taking chances.

In the passage of love, we navigate,
Through twists and turns, our destinies await.

Each encounter, a fleeting moment of bliss,
In the sweet caress of a stolen kiss.

Yet as we play this game of cat and mouse,
In the depths of our souls, love finds its house.

For in the silence between our words,
The truest emotions are always heard.

So let's continue this dance, you and I,
Underneath the vast, starlit sky.

For in this game of hide and seek we play,
Love blossoms in the most mysterious way.

By the Coffee Machine

Amid the hum of cafe chatter,
A glance shared by the coffee machine,

Eyes meet, a silent connection,
Brief, yet loaded with unspoken words.

In that fleeting moment,
Time slows, suspended,

A glimpse into another's soul,
In the midst of mundane routine.

The world rushes on around us,
But here, by the coffee machine,

A quiet affection open out,
Brief, but infinitely profound.

My cup of tea!

Sipping tea on tables far across,
In the quiet café, where time emboss,

I steal glances, though you're unaware,
In the rhythm of life, I sit and stare.

Your laughter, a melody that fills the air,
In the corner, unnoticed, I silently dare,

To dream of moments where our paths align,
Yet in this unrequited love, you'll never be mine.

As I sip my tea, lost in reverie,
I paint pictures of what could never be,

For in this distance, a chasm wide,
I'll cherish this love, silently by your side.

So I'll sip my tea, and watch you from afar,
In the sanctuary of my unspoken memoir,

For even as our tables remain apart,
In my heart, you'll always hold a part.

Cool Dashboard

When I first saw your brown eyes,
I discovered poetry,

Something similar to a software application using
telemetry for observability!

Your face appeared like a cool dashboard,
A user-friendly interface of grace.

Each feature a gauge, a metric scored,
Making it effortless to navigate your space.

In your eyes, I find real-time data,
Emotions displayed with clarity and style.

A glance, a smile—an intuitive schema, Mapping the
contours of your captivating profile.
Your voice resonates like a smooth API, Streaming
insights into my eager ears.

Each word a payload, a message to comply,
Unlocking secrets beyond mere veneers.

With you, I feel like a vigilant observer, Monitoring
heartbeats, emotions in sync.

Your presence, a dashboard I never tire, Revealing
beauty with every blink.

So, let me immerse in this interface divine, Where all
metrics trend on an upward climb,

For in your face, I find a dashboard sublime,
A captivating design in the realm.

A Character so bold!

Every time I think of you, I ponder why,
There's a mystery between us, beneath the sky.

Something unknown, something so ambiguous,
A connection full of humor, yet quite serious.

Who else would meet the same soul time and again,
In the passage of life, where paths intertwine?
A story unfolds, page after page,
as if trapped in some cage!

It's the humor of fate that brings us together,
In this cosmic comedy, where hearts tether.

Every thought of you is a chapter untold,
In my story, a character so bold

Missing part of me

In you, I sought the missing part of me,
A reflection of what I longed to see,
Yet in your absence, I began to be.

Thank you for the journey, unforeseen,
For showing me the best that lies within,
In your absence, my self-love did begin.

So here's to growth, to lessons learned with grace,
To finding beauty in the solitary space,
In loving me, I find my true embrace.

Diverse thoughts!

Intellectually divergent, yet bound by the pull,
Our thoughts soar on separate planes, full.

The gap between us vast, like stars in the night,
Yet we share the same gravity, the same light.

You dwell in realms of knowledge and insight,
While I wander through realms of emotions, in plight.
Though our paths rarely cross in understanding's
game,
We're united by the force, the Universe is yet to
claim.

Despite the distance in our mental grace,
We meet in the orbit of a one-sided embrace.

In this cosmic dance of minds so apart,
I find solace in the beating of my heart.

Empty Parking lot

Everybody looks for an empty parking lot,
But trust me, everybody actually desires to find one
under a tree!
A space where calm and comfort intertwine,
Where they can rest, and feel serene, and fine.

You find my heart an empty parking lot,
A place where you can park your emotions, untaught,
Without obligations to steer or stay,
Just a brief respite on your hurried way.

Each time you leave, a space is left behind,
A void in my heart, yet I'm always kind.

So park your emotions in my open lot,
Take what you need, and worry not.

I'll guard your secrets, and hold them tight,
In this quiet, green haven, beneath the soft twilight.

karmic Konnection

It was not the first time when I felt it.
Something happened and my heart skipped a beat,
In your presence, time itself seemed to retreat.

With every stride, you drew nearer still,
My senses enraptured, under your spell.
In your gaze, I felt a fluttering sensation,
As if destiny whispered of our Karmic Konnection.

As you closed the distance, my pulse quickened pace,
A symphony of emotions, I struggled to embrace.
For in that moment, the world seemed to fade,
Leaving just you and I, in a convoluted passage.

When you walked towards me, it felt like fate,
As if the universe conspired to orchestrate
A meeting of souls, destined to intertwine,
In the tapestry of life, yours and mine.

The seeing business

They saw me seeing you, eyes lost in a dream,
A secret unspoken, yet plain to be seen.

They saw you seeing me, a glance swift and shy,
A passing connection that soared to the sky.

In crowded moments, where time seemed to pause,
Our silent exchanges defied all the laws.

They saw us seeing each other, in a world of our own,
A story unwritten, yet perfectly known.

Two souls intertwined in the simplest of ways,
Caught in the magic of mutual gaze.

If I were you!

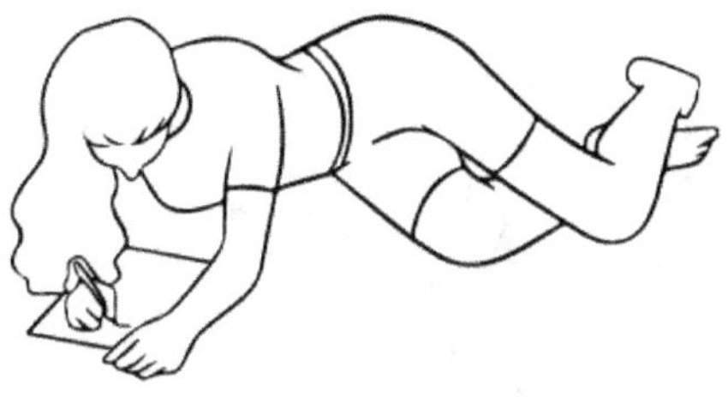

If I were you, I'd show no clue,
Appearing as if nothing happened, too.

Enjoying the attention, subtle and bright,
And the spice life was sprinkling, day and night.

I'd play it cool, with a smile so slight,
Driving and hoping to see you in some light.

Letting you overtake with heart in delight.
Finding joy in the thrill, listening to the playlist of my
choice.

I'd relish the dance, the unsaid words,
The unspoken magic that often stirs.

Living in the now, with grace so true,
If I were you, that's what I'd do.

Being Joyful

You have no idea, you have no clue
How much my thoughts revolve around you.

I avoid as much as possible your gaze,
Hoping nothing falls apart creating a mess

My heart races when you're near,
A silent longing, a quiet fear.

I steal glances when you're unaware,
Hiding feelings I cannot share.

Each word you speak, each move you make,
In my mind, they leave an endless wake.

I hope you never see my plight,
The way you light my darkest night.

For now, I'll keep my secret tight,
In dreams of you, I find my light.

Hoping time will heal or guide,
This tender pain I feel inside.

Life long tenant living rent free

In the corners of my thoughts, you remain still,
An unwelcome tenant, against my will.

Your presence, like a haunting melody,
Fills the spaces, where I long to be free.

It's a battle to evict you from my soul,
For your memory takes its heavy toll.

To ask you to vacate feels like a plea,
Yet I'm drowning in this one-sided reverie.

You're the tenant of my heart, rent-free,
Leaving me in emotional bankruptcy.

To think about you alone is a debt I can't repay,
As you make yourself at home, day by day.

But now I must bid you adieu,
For my peace of mind, I must pursue.

Though it's difficult, I must redefine,
A life where you no longer reside in mine.

Are we in sync?

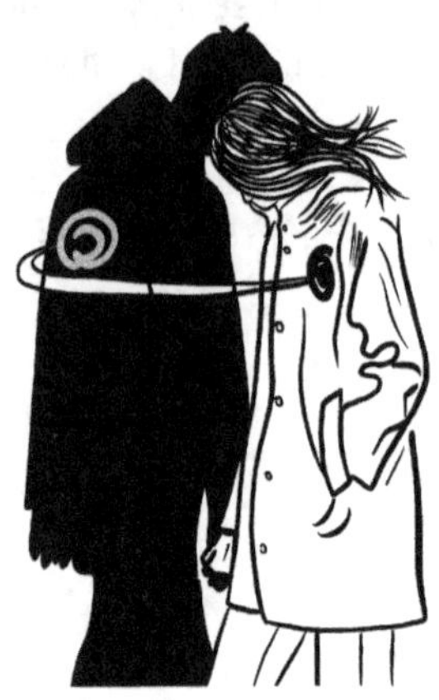

Is it the stars aligning in a celestial wink,
Or simply that we're in an unspoken sync?

Moments of magic, too strange to explain,
A call from you, just as I pick up the phone,
Thoughts mirrored perfectly, never alone.

A song plays softly, the same one you sing,
A reminder perhaps, of this mystical string.

Numbers recurring, a pattern so clear,
Evidence maybe, that you are always near.

Is it fate, destiny, or something more?
A glimpse of a truth, we can't ignore.

Threads interwoven, in life's grand design,
An intricate web, both yours and mine.

It is not necessary!

It is not necessary for him to like me back,
Nor for him to feel the same way I do.

It is not necessary for him to behave as I do,
For emotions, in its essence, is true.

No mirrored feelings need a reply,
For feelings own worth does amplify.

It lives within, not bound by two,
A solo light in shades of blue.

So I will cherish what I give,
In this world, alone I live.

Memorandum of
Understanding

Of course! It is a challenge to voice what my heart
holds deep,
Struggling to bridge the gap that seemed too steep.
I pushed beyond my limits, trying my utmost best,
To breach the silence that weighed upon my chest.

But gaps are not filled by a single hand,
It takes two to journey, to understand.
In this world of so-called social network glee,
I sought connection, but it wasn't meant to be.

The urge for reciprocation, for shared desire,
To ignite a flame that would never tire.
Yet alone, my efforts faltered, incomplete,
In this landscape where solace and longing meet.

Though I reached out, my voice lost in the void,
A testament to humanity left unenjoyed.
So I bear the weight of unspoken words unsaid,
In the chaos of feelings, where dreams are led.
Knowing now that gaps can't close with one alone,
It is better to make an agreement with self and bear
the feelings alone...

Let's keep it a secret!

Some secrets are never told, kept safe within, in the
chambers of a tender heart.
Words unspoken, like a silence reverberated in my
mind.
Some notes are never used, perhaps unheard,
Yet they resonate in the depths of the soul.

Notes that stay like a whispered word, Boundless
emotions beyond control.

Some memories never die, they linger on, stamped in
the varieties of time's embrace.

In the game of shadows and the light of dawn, They
leave a punch, a lasting trace.

And in the end, we all become stories, written in the
chapters of someone's life.

Our joys, our sorrows, our quests for glories,
Weaving narratives in the grand design of strife.

So let us embrace each passing moment,
For we are the authors of our own tales.
In the symphony of life's unfolding ornament, May
our stories resonate, where destiny prevails.

www.ingramcontent.com/pod-product-compliance
Lightning Source LLC
LaVergne TN
LVHW010950200726
843509LV00013B/2357